OWLS

OWLS

BY FERN G. BROWN

FRANKLIN WATTS
NEW YORK   LONDON   TORONTO   SYDNEY
A FIRST BOOK 1991

Cover photographs courtesy of U.S. Fish and Wildlife Service by:
Dan O'Neal and Don Pfitzer (inset)
Photographs courtesy of: Jeff Greenberg Agency: pp. 2 (Doris Friedman),
21 (Tony LaGruth); Joe McDonald: pp. 8, 13, 16, 20, 24, 27 bottom, 30,
31, 46, 50, 55; Cornell Laboratory of Ornithology: pp. 15 (Richard R.
Eakin), 17 (James Weaver), 25, 32 (both Lang Elliott), 27 top
(G. vanFrankenhuysen), 39 (Mike Hopiak), 43 (Laura Riley), 45 (R.A.
Sievers); David W. Johnson: p 35; Monkmeyer Press Photo: p. 36
(Leonard Lee Rue III).

Library of Congress Cataloging-in-Publication Data

Brown, Fern G.
    Owls / by Fern G. Brown
        p.   cm.—(A First Book)
    Includes bibliographical references and index.
    Summary: Describes the life cycle, habits and behavior, and
different species of owls.
    ISBN 0-531-20008-6
    1. Owls—Juvenile literature. [1. Owls.] I. Title.
II. Series.
QL696.S8B76   1991
598.9'7—dc20   90-13093   CIP   AC

CONTENTS

With love to my husband,
Leonard, a wise owl

The author and editors wish to express their appreciation to the following, who have been of great assistance in preparing this book: Nan Buckardt, Naturalist and Site Manager, Ryerson Conservation Area, Deerfield, Illinois; R. Bret Stahler, Director and Co-Founder, and Kim Stahler, Executive Director, the Raptor Rehabilitation Education Project, Bellefontaine, Ohio; Steve Hoddy, Director of Florida's Weeki Wachee Educational Division; and Keneitha Bryson, Jeannette Markus, Lillian Markus, and Bette Berg.

Owls may appear more intelligent
than they really are.

INTRODUCTION

Have you ever heard an owl cry out at night? The hoots and screams of those mysterious birds are sometimes scary. Yet we're so fascinated by owls, we've made them part of our fables and myths for centuries. Owls have been called wise, magical, and evil.

Are owls wise? The ancient Greeks thought so because Athena, the goddess of wisdom, favored the owl. But it's probably the owl's big, round eyes that make it look more intelligent than other birds. The truth is, owls are not as smart as geese, crows, or ravens.

Are owls magical? We have used our imagination to make them seem so. It was once thought if you ate the heart of an owl you could predict the future. Various owl parts were used as cures for sickness. Shakespeare, in his play *Macbeth,* added an owlet's wing to the witches' brew to give the witches magical powers. But that was in a play. Nobody in real life has proved that owls are truly magical.

Are owls evil? This myth might have started because most owls hunt at night, and darkness is often thought of as evil. Or some may think the owl's sharp *talons* and curved beak look evil.

So what is the truth about owls? In the past these *predators* had a bad reputation for damaging livestock and poultry. Today most people think owls should get credit for doing a good job of controlling the population of pesky insects and destroying mice and other rodents. Let's take a closer look at the *raptors* called owls.

CHAPTER 1

THE OWL FAMILY

How much do we know about the owl's beginning? Not as much as we know about the history of other birds, which lived around 150 million years ago. The remains of a large, owl-like bird turned up buried in rock about 50 million years old. After studying this *fossil,* scientists found that owls and other birds had descended from reptiles.

Later, fossils of horned and long-eared owls were found in rocks about 36 million years old. Over the next 10 million years, barn and spotted owls developed. During the last one million years or so, owls spread all over the world. These birds developed into the modern group of predators we know today.

TYPES OF OWLS

How many types of owls are there? We really aren't sure. Experts can't agree about how to divide them. Should it be by appearance? Perhaps by the shape of the face? What about the marking on the feathers, or the size of the ear openings? Scientists did their best to classify owls. They were formed into a large group, or order, of birds called *Strigiformes*.

Owls are divided into two families. In the first family are the barn owls (Tytonidae). One type of barn owl lives in North America. There are ten other kinds of barn owls throughout the world. Of the 125–140 kinds of typical owls (Strigidae) in the second family, eighteen types live in North America.

Each type of owl is given a scientific name that tells which group it is in. The name is usually taken from Latin or Greek. The first part of an owl's name tells what *genus* it belongs to. The genus is broken down further into *species*. For instance, there are many owls in the genus *Strix*. The barred owl and spotted owl are two examples. Although they look quite a bit alike, there are some differences between them. So the genus is divided into even smaller groups. The second part of an owl's scientific name tells which species it is in. The barred owl is *Strix varia* and the spotted owl is *Strix occidentalis*.

 # HABITAT

You can find owls all over the world, from northern Greenland to the southern tip of South America. They live on all continents except Antarctica.

Owls are at home in the mountains, deserts, wooded areas, fields, and in swamps. Although most owls prefer

The barred owl has a more accented series of
hoots than some other owls. It is not usually
found in the same area as the great horned owl.

wild country, those areas keep getting smaller. They have had to figure out a way to survive. Owls such as the barn and screech owls have learned to live with human beings. They nest near homes in cities and suburbs. Instead of caves, ledges, and cliffs, they live in places like barns and church steeples.

Although some owls move around, most owls stay in the same area all year round. Only a few, like the elf owl and a small saw-whet owl, go south for the winter.

 ## SIZE

Like people, owls come in assorted sizes. The elf owl, tiniest of the North American owls, is barely 6 inches (15.24 cm) long. The largest owl is the great gray owl. If you include its foot-long tail, it measures almost 3 feet (0.91 m). When this owl spreads its wings it is probably as tall or taller than you are. In between the biggest and smallest owls are slim owls with slender wings and chubby owls with rounded wings. Owl tails are usually quite short, but there are some exceptions. The hawk owl and the great gray owl have long tails.

 ## COLOR

Usually owls are gray or brown with uneven patterns of light and dark feathers. This spotted and striped coloring helps them blend in with their surroundings. Some owls, such as the snowy owl, may be almost white. They can

The northern hawk owl
is one of the few owls
with a long tail.

The snowy owl (left) and the long-eared
owl (above) blend in with their surroundings.
This makes it difficult for their enemies
and their prey to see them.

barely be seen against the snow or sand which is their habitat. Sometimes birds of the same species look different from one another. The great horned owl that lives in the north has whitish feathers but its relatives to the south are grayish and rather drab.

HOW OWLS HUNT

Most owls are *nocturnal* birds, hunting at night. A few species hunt during the day; they are called *diurnal*. There are also owls that go out at dawn and dusk when it is not too light or dark.

CHAPTER 2

WHAT ARE OWLS LIKE?

It's easy to recognize an owl. It doesn't look like any other bird. All owls sit in an upright position. They have large heads and short, thick bodies covered with fluffy feathers. Owls' eyes are big in proportion to their size. Their eyes are set close together in their broad, flat faces. Wiry feathers fan out from a sharp, hooked bill to form a *facial disk*. Owls also have powerful, curved talons. You can't tell a female from a male on sight. But when you see a pair of owls, the female is the larger one.

 ## EYES

Most American owls have yellow or orange eyes, but a few have dark brown eyes. While the eyes of most birds are on the sides of their heads, owls' eyes point forward the way ours do. It makes them look almost human. Owls can watch

This saw whet owl appears to be all eyes.

an object with both eyes—just as we can. This is called *binocular vision*. It helps them judge how far away things are, so they can swoop down and capture their prey.

Owls may have binocular vision like us, but they can't roll their eyes around in the sockets the way we do. They have to turn their heads to look sideways. Because they have extra bones in their flexible necks, these birds can turn their heads much farther in one direction than we can. After swinging its head one way, an owl can whip it back to the starting point, then turn in the opposite direction so fast that it looks like one continuous motion. How far can you turn your head to one side without moving your shoulders?

Anything behind me?
A great horned owl can take
a look.

Light enters our eyes through the *pupils,* the openings that look like dark circles in the colored part (iris) of the eyes. Owls can control the amount of light coming into their eyes by opening and closing their pupils. When it is dark, the owl can open its pupils so that they almost fill the entire eye. When there is more light, the pupils become tiny specks. Sometimes an owl will enlarge one pupil and make the other smaller. Then it can see things in the shadows and in the light at the same time.

If owls wore socks, they would probably be mismatched because owls are color-blind. They live in a black-and-white, sometimes gray, world. Seeing small details is also a problem for owls. It has to do with their light cells. Like us, these birds have two kinds of cells that receive light. They are named for their shape. *Cones* are cells that respond to strong light and react to color. *Rods* are sensitive to dim light. The reason owls can't see details or tell color is that their eyes contain many more rod-shaped cells than cone-shaped ones. In fact, they have ten times as many rod cells as we do. If it is pitch dark, owls can't really see. Nobody can. But most of the time, even on a dark night, there is some light taken in by the owl's rod cells.

 # EARS

The little "horns" sticking up on certain owls aren't ears. They are tufts of feathers. Some owls have large ear tufts and some have small ones. Many owls have no ear tufts at all. But this is not important. Ear tufts have nothing to do with hearing.

So how do owls hear? Most owls hear through ears that are long vertical slits under the feathers on either side of their heads. Each ear has a flap of loose feathers *(auriculars)* that cover the slits. The flaps are lifted when owls listen. They can move the flaps one at a time or both at the same time, in the same direction, or in different directions. If you had ear flaps your teacher could tell whether or not you were listening in class.

In many species of owls, one ear is higher, bigger, and a different shape than the other ear. Because of these differences, sound signals reach one ear a tiny fraction of a second before it reaches the other. This makes it easier for owls to tell where a sound is coming from. Some experts think the facial disk collects sound waves, and may help owls to hear better.

 ## TALONS AND BEAKS

Like other birds of prey, owls have powerful curved talons to hold and kill their victims. Their strong hooked beaks can tear flesh. After killing an animal, the owl usually will take it to a nearby tree. Insects and small animals are held in its beak. Larger animals are held in one foot. Each foot has four toes ending in the daggerlike talons. Owls can move their second toe backward and spread their talons to get a good grip on their prey.

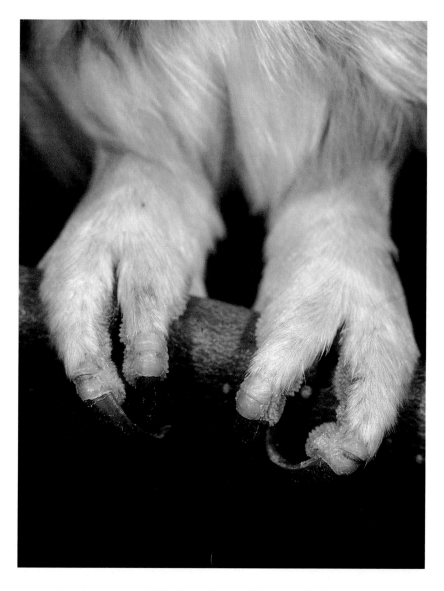

Owl toes have a firm grip for carrying
prey, and sharp talons (facing page) for killing it.

The owl's beak hooks sharply downward and looks something like a nose. Its base is hidden by soft down. Some owls have yellow beaks. Others have beaks that are black, green, or brown.

 ## FEATHERS

Owls have more feathers than most birds, but they are not very colorful. Heavy feathers keep the owls of the temperate and Arctic zones warm in winter. And feathers protect those that live in tropical climates from the hot sun.

Owls' fluffy feathers make them look much larger than they really are. Sometimes the layers of feathers are more than two inches thick—thicker than a down jacket. The owl's lower legs and upper surfaces of the toes, usually bare in birds, are often covered with feathers. Owls that live in cold regions have very thick toe feathers but tropical species have much less. Some owls have none.

The wing feathers for flying are different from owls' other feathers. They are usually long, narrow, and stiff. These feathers move the bird forward and give it the lift it needs to take it upward. The flight feathers of owls, however, are shorter and more rounded than those of other birds of the same size.

Night-hunting owls have special furry wing feathers that are fringed at the edges. The soft fringe looks like the tiny teeth of a saw-toothed knife. Most people who study owls think their fringe is what makes the owls fly so quietly.

Adult owls, like many other birds, shed their feathers and grow new ones every year. This is called *molting.* Owls usually begin to molt late in the summer. The molting process takes several weeks and is generally over by the time winter comes.

 ## FIGHTING ENEMIES

Many birds, such as crows and jays, dislike owls. Hawks are also enemies of owls. Sometimes human beings are too.

How does the owl protect itself and its family when it senses danger? Most owls can sit absolutely still in a tree

The serated edge of owls' flight wings keeps air from making too much noise as it passes over the wings.

This burrowing owl looks angry—it was threatened at its nest.

and play dead. Because they are like the color of a tree trunk, they are hard to spot. When long-eared or screech owls sense an intruder, they can play a trick. Sitting erect, they close their big, round eyes into narrow slits. Then they straighten their ear tufts, and pull their feathers tightly against their bodies. No longer fluffy, feathery owls, they now look like sticks!

Barn owls, great horned owls, and others do just the opposite. They pull themselves up to look much bigger than they are. With outspread wings circling over their heads, they hiss and snap their beaks at intruders. I wouldn't want to meet one of those owls in the woods on a dark night. Would you?

The pygmy and a few other owls have feathers on the backs of their heads that form fierce-looking masks. Enemies that come up behind these owls see what seem to be two enormous eyes staring at them. They are soon frightened away. If owls can't scare off an intruder they will fight with their wings. A word of advice—don't ever anger an owl when its young are in or around the nest.

CHAPTER 3

OWL HABITS

Owls may not fly as fast as other predators, but they don't have to. Their silence and the dark keep them hidden from their prey. When an owl swoops down with its legs shooting forward, it very seldom misses the mark. And once its powerful talons grab the prey, it almost never lets go.

FOOD

Owls help farmers by eating rodents that damage crops. Rodents are important food for owls. A large owl eats three or four mice or rats every day. It usually swallows a rodent whole. The owl menu also includes animals such as squirrels, rabbits, and skunks. Bigger owls often eat ducks and pigeons too. Some species catch fish for dinner. Others also eat snakes, lizards, and bats. Small owls feed on a variety of insects such as beetles and spiders, and also on frogs and small birds.

Lizards and rats are
common meals for owls.

With the help of powerful digestive juices, owls are able to digest most of the food they eat. The parts they can't digest (such as feathers, bones, and teeth), are pressed into a small bundle called a *pellet*. It takes about eight hours to form a pellet. Then it is forced up from the owl's stomach through the mouth with certain pumping movements of the head and neck. Some pellets are as small as your thumb. Larger pellets over 4 inches (10.16 cm) long and 2 inches (5.08 cm) wide have also been found where owls have been roosting. Usually the size of the owl determines the size of the pellet. By taking an owl pellet apart you can see what an owl has eaten.

An owl pellet reveals an owl's diet and is also an indication that an owl is near.

OWL TALK

Most owls stay in the same territory all year. Those that *migrate* tend to return to the previous year's territory at breeding time. Owls hoot to attract mates, and they use cries, hoots, and screeches to warn rivals to keep away. Other owl sounds have been described as snores, coughs, and screams.

 ## FINDING A MATE

In late winter or early spring the male owl begins to look for a mate. His special mating hoots and screeches echo throughout his territory. It may go on all night. When a female of his species answers (each species has its own cry), their courtship begins.

The male may bring the female some food. It is as if he wants to show her that he is a good hunter. In some species the male fluffs out his feathers and jumps about as if he's dancing. When the female shows she is willing to become his mate, the male hops on her back. Each bird has an opening under the tail that goes into a common holding area. It is part of the digestive tract, and is used for reproduction and getting rid of waste. The two openings are pressed together, and the male owl's sperm fertilizes the eggs inside the female. Now the pair must prepare a nesting place for the owlets that will soon be born. Once paired, owls may stay together for years, or even for life. And owls live a long time. Some large owls live for over fifteen years.

Owls are not the best nest builders. That's probably why they look for a ready-made place for the female to lay her eggs. A pair of owls will often use a woodpecker hole in a tree for their nest.

One of the species that sometimes builds its own nest is the giant great gray owl. Yet you can hardly call it a nest. Set high in a tree, it's often nothing more than a pile of twigs and grass.

Female owls lay their eggs at different times of the year, depending on the climate. There could be from two to thirteen white, nearly round eggs, although the average is about four. After the female lays the first egg, she may not lay another for two or three days. It could be a week or two before she is finished.

In order for eggs to hatch they must be *incubated.* In most species, as soon as there is an egg in the nest, the female sits on it to keep it warm. The male usually hunts for food. Each night he brings his mate several small animals to eat. In some species the male and female take turns incubating the eggs.

In three to five weeks all the eggs are hatched. The young are different sizes. Born with closed eyes and few feathers, they look like white puffballs. As soon as they work their way out of the shell you can hear their "hunger cry." It ranges from a whimper to a noise like what you hear when you sip through a straw at the bottom of a drink.

In some species, males bring the food to feed the babies. In others the male and female take turns hunting.

This baby great horned owl is less than twelve hours old.

While the chicks are young, one parent always stays in the nest to protect them. Small prey are fed to the babies whole. Large prey are torn into pieces by the parents and passed to the nestlings.

The first birds to hatch are usually larger and stronger than the others. Because of their size and strength, these birds usually get the most to eat. The last birds hatched are likely to be the weakest. If food is scarce, the larger birds

These baby barn owls were born after incubating for 32 to 34 days.

may kill and eat the smaller, weaker nestlings. In that way a few strong birds will leave the nest instead of many weaklings that may not survive on their own. This may seem cruel, but if the nestlings were fed equally, they might all starve to death.

About a week after hatching, depending on the species, the nestling's eyes open. The bird is now covered with soft down. Nestlings stay in the nest for four to six weeks. The adults search the territory for food every night. As the young grow it gets harder and harder to find enough food to feed them. Sometimes the adults have to make twenty or more trips a night. Although owlets usually leave the nest before they can fly, they don't go far. While the young are in or around the nest, the parents use all the tricks they know to scare enemies away.

During the next six to nine weeks the young birds gradually lose their soft down and grow stiff feathers. They learn to hunt for themselves. How the owlets have grown! It won't be long until they fly away, stake out a territory, and raise their own family.

CHAPTER 4

SOME INTERESTING OWLS

There are about 9,000 kinds of birds, and 125–140 kinds of owls. This chapter will tell you about some interesting Strigiformes.

 ## THE BARN OWL (*TYTO ALBA*)

A friend brought Leonard J. Soucy, Jr. an abandoned nest with three barn-owl eggs. Although he watched over the eggs and kept them warm, Leonard did not think they would hatch. But one of them did! He named it Lady. Leonard fed and cared for the young owl which he laughingly said looked more like a punk-rock star than a bird. The owl became attached to Leonard, and would probably have been surprised to learn that Leonard was not its mother. Leonard was surprised too when Lady turned out to be a male.

Lady was an *imprint*. Imprinting happens during a short, critical period soon after hatching. Because Lady depended on Leonard for food and care during his early life, Lady couldn't tell the difference between a human being and one of his own species. Lady was Leonard's companion and prize educational exhibit for fourteen years.

Barn owls are found in every continent except Antarctica. They have strange-looking faces. Instead of being rounded like most owls, their faces are heart-shaped. That's why this owl is sometimes called the monkey-faced owl.

You can clearly see the heart-shaped faces of these common barn owls.

The underside of the barn owl's body is stark white. It looks rather ghostlike gliding through the night. It would be spooky to see a barn owl fly over your head. Its eerie screams could send shivers down your spine.

Barn owls are about 18 inches long (45.72 cm), and have a 3-foot (0.91 m) wingspan. Females lay five to seven eggs over the course of a few days. This night hunter with its sharp hearing is a mousetrap with wings. It is said that a pair of barn owls can catch more rodents than a dozen cats. Despite their name, barn owls don't always find nests in barns. They like hollow trees too, and sometimes they make their homes in a bell tower or an old windmill. Recently some barn owls were discovered nesting behind a drive-in movie screen!

THE GREAT HORNED OWL (*BUBO VIRGINIANUS*)

One day a farmer found a sick great horned owl lying in the middle of his chicken coop. The poor bird was starving and too weak to hunt. Newly built buildings nearby had destroyed the owl's territory. The farmer took it to Kim Stahler, Executive Director of the Raptor Rehabilitation and Education Project in Bellefontaine, Ohio. Kim received fifteen sick or injured great horned owls that month. But she is happy to report that they have all been nursed back to health and released into the wild.

Recently in Florida a great horned owlet fell out of a crude hollow-tree nest. It wasn't able to fly or hunt. A hiker found the baby owl lying on the ground shivering. She brought it to Steve Hoddy, Director of Education in the Bird Department of Weeki Wachee Spring. Steve felt sorry for the ugly little bird he named Shadow. Because of an infection, Shadow had grown no down or feathers. When he was put in with other owls, they ganged up on him, so Steve had to raise Shadow by hand. One day, just like the ugly duckling in the fairy tale, Shadow began to grow feathers. He turned into a beautiful great horned owl! But he will never be released into the wild as Kim's birds were. Shadow has not learned to hunt. In the wild he would probably be killed, or would starve to death.

The great horned owl, often called the "feathered tiger of the air," is one of the largest and fiercest of owls. It measures 18–25 inches (46–64 cm) from the tip of its bill to the end of its tail and has a wingspread of 35–55 inches (89–140 cm). Yet this big bird weighs no more than a stewing hen (3–5 lbs) [approx. 1.35–2.25 kg]. Great horned owls have very large "horns" (ear tufts) which give them their name. A master night hunter, the great horned owl's yellow, saucerlike eyes are at least twenty-five times more sensitive to light than ours are.

The great horned owl can live anywhere—in trees or on rocky ledges. It is found in almost every part of North and South America except the far north. The northern great horned owl has whitish feathers while its relatives to the south are brown or grayish.

Great horned owls make their homes in abandoned nests of large birds such as crows or hawks. Females lay from two to four eggs, about the size of jumbo chicken

41

eggs. The male and female take turns keeping the eggs warm. These owls look for mates and nests early—at the end of February or beginning of March. Can you picture a great horned owl, its large tufts covered with snow, its yellow eyes gleaming, sitting on a nest keeping the eggs warm?

THE SCREECH OWL (*OTUS ASIO*)

It was about two in the morning at Keneitha Bryson's home in Waynesville, North Carolina. She woke up and heard crying. The baby was fast asleep. What was that long, quavering, cooing sound? Looking out the window, Keneitha saw six little gray screech owls sitting on her bird feeder! Six pairs of yellow eyes stared at her for a minute. With heads stretched up and feathers drawn tightly about their bodies, they didn't look much like birds. Suddenly, the six little owls turned their heads in unison. They seemed to go around in a complete circle. What a funny sight!

The screech owl is probably the best-known small owl. Despite its name, it really doesn't screech. Of its many calls the most familiar is the quavering series of cooing notes Keneitha heard.

There are about twenty kinds of North American screech owls. They are found everywhere from Alaska to northern Mexico. About 10 inches (25 cm) high, they are the only small owls with ear tufts. Most screech owls nest in hollow trees. They eat small rodents, insects, and birds. The families usually consist of four to six young.

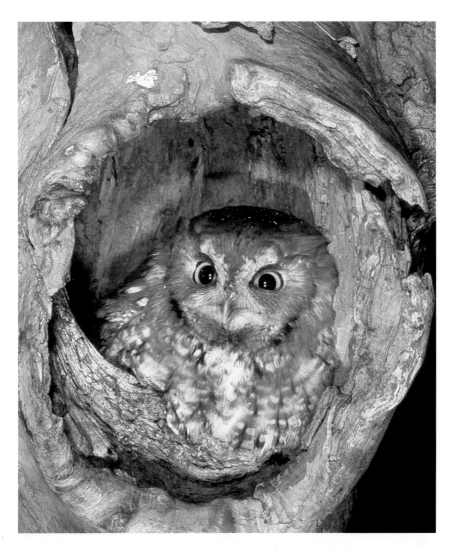

This eastern screech owl has made its nest in a hollow tree. The screech owls have a varied diet; they'll eat beetles, frogs, fish, moths, and bats.

BURROWING OWL (*SPEOTYTO CUNICULARIA*)

Seven-year-old Jordan Gilbert was on a nature hike when he heard a violent hissing sound coming from a hole in the ground. A rattlesnake! He jumped back. The naturalist leading the hike explained that it was not a rattlesnake. A burrowing owl was warning Jordan to keep away from its nest. An owl's nest in a gopher hole?

This brown-and-white spotted bird is a special kind of owl. It lives in the wild and is usually active during the day. The females often lay eight or nine eggs, and the parents will raise their young underground in abandoned holes or burrows. The nesting chamber is often at the end of a long, twisting tunnel.

Burrowing owls hunt insects and small animals, including rodents called voles. When hunting is good, these owls gather food and store it. This is an unusual habit for an owl. Although most other owls live alone in winter, perhaps twenty burrowing owls will spend winter together in one burrow, sharing the stored food.

OTHER INTERESTING OWLS

The beautiful **snowy owl** (*Nyctea scandiaca*) is a huge bird with bright yellow eyes and an almost white body. This owl's leg feathers are so thick they look like a pair of fur boots.

Burrowing owls have long legs and live
in the ground. In areas where no other
animals have abandoned their holes,
burrowing owls will dig their own homes.

This snowy owl was photographed in Canada's arctic tundra.

Home to the snowy owl is the frozen Arctic tundra—a flat, treeless area just south of the polar region. Snowy owls lay their eggs in nests on top of mounds of earth pushed up by the frost. Because they live in the land of the midnight sun, there is a long, Arctic summer, when snowy owls have no choice but to hunt during the day. When winter comes, the sun leaves for six months, and they hunt in the dark. These owls feed mostly on lemmings, which are ratlike rodents. When food is plentiful the snowy owls lay many eggs. If there is a shortage of lemmings, however, the owls may not lay any eggs. This happens every three to five years, and when it does the snowy owls fly south for the winter. Many are shot by hunters; some starve. When spring comes, the surviving owls fly home to the tundra. As the lemming population increases, the cycle of the snowy owl—plenty to eat, lemming shortage, and flying south—begins again.

The drab northern **spotted owl** (*Strix occidentalis*) is interesting because it lives in the dense old-growth forests (trees at least 250 years old) of the northwestern United States and southwestern Canada. While most American owls have yellow or orange eyes, this shy 14-inch (36 cm) owl has dark brown eyes. By day, the spotted owl roosts in tall trees or crevices in steep canyon walls. By night, it stalks flying squirrels and red tree voles.

Weighing less than an ounce, the tiny **elf owl** (*Micra-thene whitneyi*) is one of the smallest owls in the world. These little birds live in the southwestern United States. Every year they migrate, spending summer in one place and winter in another. Mostly a night hunter, this owl

OWL FACTS

COMMON NAME SCIENTIFIC NAME	CHARACTERISTICS	HABITAT	APPROX. SIZE IN INCHES (AND CENTIMETERS)
barn owl (*Tyto alba*)	heart-shaped face, white underside	every continent except Antarctica; hollow trees, barns, towers, steeples	18 (46 cm)
great horned owl (*Bubo virginianus*)	long ear tufts, yellow saucerlike eyes	every part of N. & S. America except far north; trees and rocky ledges	18–25 (46–64 cm)
N. American screech owl (*Otus asio*)	only small owl with ear tufts, red or gray feathers, mottled or barred	from Alaska to New Mexico; hollow trees	10 (25 cm)
burrowing owl (*Speotyto cunicularia*)	brown-and-white spotted, few feathers	western U.S.; in underground burrows	10 (25 cm)
snowy owl (*Nyctea scandiaca*)	bright yellow eyes, mostly white body, thick leg feathers	frozen Arctic tundra; migrates in winter	20 (50 cm)
spotted owl (*Strix occidentalis*)	brown eyes, yellow beak, light breast spotted with brown	northwestern U.S. & southwestern Canada; old-growth forests	18 (46 cm)
elf owl (*Micrathene whitneyi*)	smallest, short tail, weighs less than an ounce	southwestern U.S. and other warm areas; woodpecker holes in giant desert cactus	6 (15 cm)
great gray owl (*Strix nebulosa*)	largest N. American, big facial disk, no ear tufts, fluffy feathers	northern U.S., fir and spruce trees	36 (91 cm) (incl. 12-in. [30 cm] tail)

feeds on grasshoppers, spiders, and insects. The elf owl usually prefers nesting in holes made by woodpeckers and flickers in the giant saguaro cacti of the desert. The sharp spines of the cactus help protect the elf owls from their enemies.

Probably the largest of the eighteen North American owls is the **great gray owl** (*Strix nebulosa*). Although it is more than five times as tall as the elf owl, it weighs only 3 pounds (1.35 kg). You may think great grays look odd because they have no ear tufts. Their soft, fluffy feathers and large facial disks make up for it. Great gray owls live in the north in heavily wooded areas of fir and spruce trees. They are good hunters. Their prey is mostly forest rodents but they may also feed on large birds such as crows.

CHAPTER 5

ARE YOU A WISE OWL?

Do you know that it is against the law to kill an owl or any native bird? **Do you know** that because spotted owls live in old trees, environmentalists have demanded that those forests be protected so the owls can survive? People in the timber industry claim that if they can't cut down old trees, it will be bad for the forest products industry. Both sides are fighting it out in court. **Do you know** that since the early 1980s biologists have been strapping miniature radio *transmitters* on the backs of spotted owls? They send signals back to the scientists telling what is happening to the owls. We want to know if the owls are *endangered.*

WHO CARES ABOUT OWLS?

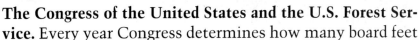

The Congress of the United States and the U.S. Forest Service. Every year Congress determines how many board feet of old timber growth will be sold. Then the U.S. Forest Service decides which areas should be cut. A joint Congressional committee recently approved a compromise plan to allow old-growth logging for one year.

The Raptor Rehabilitation Education Project of Bellefontaine, Ohio. One of many nonprofit raptor rehabilitation projects in the U.S., the purpose of this project is to preserve birds of prey. Run by volunteers, the Project sets up programs to educate people about raptors. It also cares for and releases injured birds into the wild.

Leonard J. Soucy, Jr., of Millington, New Jersey. An expert on barn owls, Mr. Soucy is the founder and director of The Raptor Trust. It is a nonprofit rehabilitation center for injured and abandoned birds of prey. Soucy is trying to show people there is a place for raptors in our society.

The National Wildlife Association distributes free educational materials with information about predators. Among the materials are TV programs, books, filmstrips, and tapes. This association also has a staff of experts who keep track of what's going on in predator research, laws, and court actions around the country.

Florida's Weeki Wachee Spring is one of the free-flying bird shows that feature owls. Working with the Audubon Society Rehabilitation Center, it is part of an educational project. While sick or injured imprints are nursed back to health and trained for the show, skilled trainers prepare wild birds to return to the wild.

TAKE AN OWL PROWL. At Ryerson Conservation Area in Deerfield, Illinois, you can sign up for an owl hike. It takes place at night, close to a full moon. Here's what you do. First of all, dress warm. Don't take a flashlight. Your eyes will get used to the dark. After a short introduction from the naturalist guide you'll be ready to go. Walk quietly. The hike at Ryerson is usually a circular mile in an area of oaks, hickories, and evergreens where owls have been seen. The naturalist will "call in the owls." This means imitating the owl's call or playing a recording of that owl's voice.

You're apt to get an answer from a male great horned owl. He will call back as if to say, "Stay out of my territory." When the naturalist sends the call for the second time, the owl will usually come in to see who is there. Be especially quiet. Listen and look in the owl's direction. If you see the owl, the tape is not played again. Otherwise it is played several times until the owl flies into view. Now the great horned is puffing himself up to look larger. He is clacking his beak. It sounds like a snap of the fingers. Don't be afraid, he won't attack you. He is only trying to defend himself by saying, "Hit the road, buddy."

After you've seen the owl, the group will hike back to the visitor's center. Why not plan your own owl prowl?

TAKE APART AN OWL PELLET. When you are on an owl prowl, you'll find pellets on the ground under the owl's nest. Take one apart carefully. Make a list of the things you find inside. You may see the skull of a tiny mouse, or its jaw, teeth, leg, or hip bone. You might find the remains of a small bird. If you can't find an owl pellet, perhaps the nature center will give you one.

VISIT A BIRDS-OF-PREY SHOW. Look in the telephone book and see if there is one in your area.

LOOK FOR AN OWL STORY IN THE SNOW. Search when the snow is wet, and no more than 3 inches (7.62 cm) deep. You may see a tiny mouse footprint. Mice hop, leaving a 4-foot (1.22 m) pattern with front feet landing side by side. If the trail ends abruptly, look for signs of an owl. Its wings may be outlined in the snow.

MAKE A BARN OWL NEST. Construct a 24-inch (60-cm) -long wooden box for a barn owl's nest. Make the roof so it slightly overlaps a hole seven inches (17 cm) in diameter on one side. Attach the box to a pole or tree in an open field.

 # THINGS NOT TO DO

If you find a baby owl on the ground, don't take it home. Owlets live on the ground for days or weeks until they leave to hunt. Their parents tend to them while they are on the ground. Besides, it is against the law to keep an owl without a special permit.

Don't use poison to get rid of mice and rats. Many barn owls die young because of eating poisoned rodents. The

An eastern screech owl leaves its box nest.

poison makes some rodents weak, and it's easy for owls to catch them. If most of the owls have died because of eating poisoned, weak rodents, how will we keep the rodent population under control?

 ## THE FUTURE OF OWLS

Because owls kill farm animals in order to survive, they have been treated badly in the past. But now most people are aware that owls kill many more mice than they kill chickens or ducks. If owls can find wild prey they will usually stay away from farms. Yet because we are building more homes, shopping centers, and office buildings, we are destroying the owl's territories and food supply. And when we remove old and dead trees from forests, we are taking away their nesting sites. If we want these raptors to survive, we must protect them and save their territories so they can live.

GLOSSARY

Auriculars. Flaps of loose feathers that cover an owl's ear slits.

Binocular vision. Able to see two images, one from each eye.

Cones. Cells in the eye sensitive to bright light.

Diurnal. Active during the day.

Endangered species. An organism in danger of becoming extinct.

Facial disk. Circle of stiff feathers around an owl's face.

Fossil. Trace of an organism of a past age.

Genus. A group in the scientific classification system made up of species that have many characteristics in common.

Imprint. Process by which a bird identifies its parents, a nest site, or a food source. It is a unique form of learning that occurs during a sensitive period after hatching. It is thought to be irreversible.

Incubate. Sit on laid eggs to keep them warm so they'll hatch.

Migrate. Move from one area to another to find food or stay for a while in a different climate.

Molting. Loss of a set of feathers on a regular seasonal basis, and their replacement by new feathers.

Nestling. A young bird that has not abandoned the nest.

Nocturnal. Active at night.

Pellet. A bundle of animal or insect parts the owl can't digest.

Predator. Kills and eats other animals for food.

Pupils. The part of the eye that expands or contracts to let different levels of light into the eye.

Raptors. Birds of prey, such as the owl, eagle, and hawk.

Rods. Cells in the eyes that are sensitive to dim light.

Species. Smallest group in scientific classification. Those in same species are very similar with only minor differences.

Strigiformes. The order that owls belong to.

Talons. Sharp, curved claws of a predator.

Transmitter. An instrument that sends a signal by wire or radio.

FOR FURTHER READING

Catchpole, Clive. *Owls.* New York: McGraw–Hill Book Co., 1977.

Hoke, Helen and Pitt, Valerie. *Owls.* New York: Franklin Watts, 1975.

Lavine, Sigmund A. *Wonders of the Owl World.* New York: Dodd, Mead and Co., 1971.

Sadoway, Margaret Wheeler. *Owls.* Minneapolis: Lerner Publications Co., 1981.

Stone, Lynn M. *The Great Horned Owl.* Mankato, Minnesota: Crestwood House, 1987.

Zim, Herbert S. *Owls.* New York: William Morrow and Co., 1977.

FOR MORE INFORMATION

You can write to:

Raptor Rehabilitation Education Project
P.O. Box 895
Bellefontaine, OH 43311

The Raptor Trust
Millington, NJ 07946

National Wildlife Federation
1400 16th St. N.W.
Washington, DC 20036-2266

Florida's Weeki Wachee Educational Division
P.O. Box 97
Brooksville, FL 34298-0097

Ryerson Conservation Area
21950 Riverwoods Rd.
Deerfield, IL 60015

INDEX

ABOUT
THE AUTHOR

Fern G. Brown is a former teacher and an established writer of both fiction and nonfiction for children and young adults. Mrs. Brown lives in Riverwoods, Illinois, with her husband, Leonard. This is her seventh book for Franklin Watts.